ISBN 9781502404404

Published at Sonrise Chapel in Everett,
Washington. © 2011 Sonrise Chapel.
All rights reserved.

Editing by Pat Burke, Scott Smith & Dan Hammer

Graphics and finishing by Debra Werdell

a New Identity
Workbook by:
John Hammer

The Identity, Authority and Privileges We Have in Christ

Table of Contents

Introduction

The identity and authority we have in Christ

Welcome to, *a New Identity – The Identity, Authority and Privileges we have in Christ*. The powerful truths that are about to be opened will excite your spirit and help you embrace your true identity in Christ. Embrace it solidly and your whole world will change.

A human mindset is shaped by two important factors: our personal view of God and how we view ourselves. This book will be concerned primarily with what the Bible teaches about who believers are and how to see yourself as a believer in Jesus. These two perceptions meet at your core. How you see God often determines the way you see yourself and vice versa. The good news of Jesus Christ was not merely designed to get you into heaven but to transform your life and set your perspective as well. When you study the Bible and believe what it says about your identity, you will begin to understand the deep, incredible love God has for you.

The actual phrases "in Christ," "in Christ Jesus," "in the Lord" or "in Him" are found over 100 times in the Bible. Once you believe Jesus is the Son of God, Savior and Lord of your soul, you are "in Christ."

This book is all about discovering who you are, it is not a book about selfishness. Christians are called to focus outwardly by loving God and loving others. Often believers don't fully know or understand the love God has for His children. Not knowing or feeling loved by God can hinder success to "love back" in relationship with Him and others. 1 John 4:19, says that, *"We love Him because He first loved us."* This book is about being free from your old self in order that you are able to freely love God and others.

Action steps

1. Establish a time and place with your coach-discipler for the first meeting.

   ## Coach-discipler information

   Name _____

   Phone _____

   Email _____

   Time _____

   Location _____

2. Study your first lesson.

Chapter One

In Christ (Part 1)

"Therefore, if anyone is in Christ, he is a new creation; old things have passed away; behold, all things have become new." 2 Corinthians 5:17

The need for a new identity

As sinners we have lost our true identity. Romans 3:23 says, *"for all have sinned and fall short of the glory of God."* We are not able to be in a relationship with God, nor do we have a clear understanding of ourselves.

In Genesis 3, it's clear what happened when man and woman sinned by disobeying God. First of all, mankind's unbroken and loving relationship with God was fractured through disobedience. Secondly, all people born after Adam would be sinners too.

What does Romans 5:18, say about mankind in relationship to Adam's sin? _____

_____

_____

Thirdly, man no longer saw himself the way God had intended him to.

Read Genesis 3:8. What did Adam and Eve do after they sinned against God? _____

_____

Their reaction reveals what they experienced for the first time: guilt, shame, fear and insecurity. When man listened to Satan instead of to God they sinned and exchanged their true identity. Their image of themselves and God was tainted because they believed and acted out a lie.

Fast forward several thousand years when Jesus showed up on the scene. He talked to one man named Nicodemus who was a religious leader.

What does Jesus say to Nicodemus in John 3:3 about what is necessary for man? _____

_____

_____

_____

Spiritual rebirth is paramount. It is necessary to be born again to have a relationship with God and enter His kingdom. You must be reborn as a new creation because the old self cannot see the way God sees, or have relationship with Him.

Read 2 Corinthians 5:17. What does it say about those who are "in Christ?" _____

_____

_____

When you become spiritually reborn, you become a brand new creation. You are no longer that old sinner. You have a new identity.

Go to Romans 5:18-19. What do these verses say about the contrast between those who live from Adam's line and those who live from the line of Christ? _____

_____

_____

All are born in the line of Adam as sinners. But when one comes to believe in Jesus and experiences new birth they are reborn in the line of Jesus as a son/daughter and saint. Believers are no longer limited to the effects of natural birth and life as sinners. In Christ, believers get the opposite of what is deserved through Adam.

Action steps

1. Briefly add to the chart below with your past identity and what God says about you now in your new life.

Your identity

Through Adam	Through Jesus
sinner	saint and son/daughter
orphan	adopted
no purpose	purpose
fear	loved
insecure	secure
anxiety	peace
guilt	forgiven
shame	accepted
hopelessness	joint-heir
Through Adam	**Through Jesus**

slavery	redemption
Hell	Heaven
confusion	order
brokenness	restoration
isolation	family

2. Memorize 2 Corinthians 5:17.

3. Read through the appendix, *"Affirmations of Who I am in Christ."* Read it everyday and read it out loud. This will begin to help you line up with what God says about you.

Are *you* born again?

As you read earlier, it is absolutely imperative that you be "born again" to enter God's Kingdom. All the promises in the Bible discussed in this book are only true for those who have new life in Christ, where Jesus is their true king. Being born again isn't automatic if you grew up in church, have Christian parents or repeated a little prayer. New life in Christ begins when God, by the Holy Spirit, awakens a once-dead spirit to life. First there must be personal repentance from sin and belief in what Jesus did through the cross and resurrection.

If you have "asked" Jesus to be in your life but there has been no change in your heart, you may need to experience the new birth. It's not difficult to receive God's gift of salvation, but it's important to realize if you have truly received it or not. If Christ has been part of your life but not actually the Lord of your life and if you desire to know God and let Him lead you then He is working in your heart and drawing you to Himself. Be confident of this: that He wants you to know Him more than you desire to know Him. Take some time and pray the following if you have not yet made Jesus your Lord and Savior.

Pray this

Heavenly Father, thank you for sending Jesus to die for my sin. Thank You for loving me so much. I believe in You Jesus. I believe You died, shed Your blood and rose from the dead for me. I ask You now to cleanse me of all my sin (take time to confess specifics that come to your mind). Thank You for washing all my sin away, the ones I remember and the ones I don't. I choose to turn away from sin and turn my life to You. Be the Lord and leader of my life. Have all of me. Empower me Holy Spirit to follow Jesus everyday. Thank You for new life that starts now and lasts forever. Thank You for saving me. In Jesus' name, amen.

Chapter 2

In Christ (Part 2)

"For you died, and your life is hidden with Christ in God." Colossians 3:3

What happens to my "old self"?

When you become a new creation in Christ Jesus, as read in Colossians 3:3, your old self is dead. You are no longer the same person. Sin no longer rules and dominates your life. A dead man cannot do anything, let alone sin.

Read Romans 6:1-7. What happened to your old self? _____

_____

_____

_____

What must you do as a believer in Jesus to identify with the death of your old self? _____

_____

_____

What happens to your relationship with sin as a result of dying to your old self?_____

_____

_____

_____

Read 1 Corinthians 6:9-11. List the unrighteous people found here that will not inherit the kingdom of God. _____

_____

_____

_____

_____

_____

In 1 Corinthians 6:11, God refers to these unrighteous people using an identity in the past tense, "were." The world labels people permanently and often does not believe people can actually change. The miracle of Christian salvation is that no matter what the old self was, each can be changed and not be held by the labels of the past.

What does 1 Corinthians 6:11 say about you now as a believer in Christ? _____

_____

Sanctified[1] – to make holy, consecrated, purified

Justified[2] – to render, show or regard as: just, innocent, free and righteous

What were some of the labels of your past life? _____

_____

_____

_____

_____

_____

What are the labels God has given to you in their place?

_____

_____

_____

_____

Read Colossians 1:13-14. According to these verses what was the old kingdom called? _____

_____

Are you part of the old kingdom? _____

What is the new kingdom called? _____

_____

Do you belong to the new kingdom? _____

In this new kingdom what do believers have from Jesus (verse 14)? _____

_____

_____

Your new relationship with God

Read Romans 6:8-10. According to these verses, believers are not only dead to sin and their old self, but now are what?_____

_____

_____

Not just dead to sin anymore; believers are now alive to God. Mankind was created for relationship with God. Believers are no longer under God's judgment, but have found a place of favor in His eyes.

Read Romans 8:1. Now in Christ, what is no longer upon a believer's life? _____

_____

_____

God does not condemn you. He is not against you, He is for you. Read Romans 8:31-39.

What type of situations and things does God help believers conquer as seen in these verses? _____

_____

_____

_____

Meditate on it for a minute. God loves you and once you are in Christ, you will experience love from the Creator of the universe. Your Almighty God has you on His mind. You are loved!

Read 1 John 4:16-19. Describe who God is according to this passage._____

_____

What is gone from your life if you "abide or remain in God?" __

_____

_____

God's relationship with mankind is based on love without fear. Death is no longer something to fear because God made you

His child. As Jesus is now, so are you in this world. How can this be? The next chapter will be dedicated to exploring some of what the Bible says about being a son or daughter of God. This is absolutely incredible. In the past those living apart from God were as rebellious orphans. Now His sons and daughters are truly alive, restored in right relationship and belonging to God.

A new heart

Read Ezekiel 11:19-20, Ezekiel 36:26-27, and Jeremiah 31:33-34. What do these verses say that God will do for believers? _____

_____

_____

_____

Believers get a brand new heart from God. The "new covenant" is based upon grace. The "old covenant," or law God gave to Moses was based on works. Mankind had to try and save himself. He/she had to work hard at obeying God's law in order to earn God's love. It was required to live under the law and its sacrifices in order to cover personal sin. It was a great struggle to press for righteousness under the law and have personal sin "passed over" by God.

Ezekiel was speaking forward to present day, in a time where through faith in Jesus, God would give a new heart to His people. God designed this new heart with a desire to follow His law from the inside out. God's love inside a new heart comes with freedom. You are free to *choose to* obey Him because you are already loved. No longer do you *have to* obey to earn God's love, but motivation shifts away from a desire to save yourself. Believers have God working through their hearts, where trust is consistently put in His ability to save and lead.

Read Ephesians 2:8-9. What do these verses teach about your salvation? _____

_____

_____

_____

Your salvation is by God's grace. Read Titus 2:11-12. What does this teach about the grace of God? _____

_____

_____

_____

_____

It is God's grace that saves and teaches you to stay away from ungodly things. The new heart God gives is equipped to keep you away from evil and do what God says is right. New identity in Christ produces a heart motivated by God's grace and empowered to live a right life. It is very important to avoid sin, but without understanding this new identity it is normal to try and avoid sin by one's own strength. Realize this: as God changes you on the inside you are strengthened to make right choices on the outside.

Your new relationship with others

Read 1 John 3:14. How do you know that your "old self" is dead?_____

_____

_____

Along with a new nature comes a heart change and a new set of desires of the heart. Motivations also change, but the main sign of a new creation experience is changed relationships. That is, a developing love for people.

Action steps

Spend some time thanking God that He has forgiven your sin, that you are dead to your old life, that you are alive to God and that you have a new heart motivated by God's grace!

1. If you have not yet been baptized in water, you have not fully obeyed Jesus and according to Romans 6, you are most likely going to have a difficult time seeing God's transformation in your heart. So get water baptized.

    What date will you be baptized? _____

2. Memorize Colossians 3:3._____

3. Read through the appendix, "*Affirmations of Who I am in Christ.*" Read it everyday and read it out loud. This will begin to help you line up with what God says about you.

Chapter 3

Sonship

"But as many as received Him, to them He gave the right to become children of God, to those who believe in His name: who were born, not of blood, nor of the will of the flesh, nor of the will of man, but of God." John 1:12-13

God gives believers an incredible position in Christ. He calls them sons.

Sonship is not about gender. The Bible refers to both men and women who have this right. Sonship has to do with a spiritual identity and the blessings that result. There is truly only one Savior of the world, the only begotten Son of God, Jesus Christ. No one can be equal to Him, but He does share the benefits He has from the Father with His children.

Your Father in Heaven

Jesus taught to pray, *"Our Father in heaven,"* in Matthew 6:9. What an amazing relationship to be able to call God your Father. God is far different from earthly fathers. Sometimes people have difficulty relating to God as a Father if their own dad was not a good example of the Father in heaven.

In natural birth one is born into sin through their natural family and unable to relate with God. As explained in the first chapter, each must be born again. When born again by your heavenly Father, you will see your new Father has the best in store for you. Don't allow an earthly father to set limitations on the direction of your life!

Jesus said in *John 14:9, "He who has seen Me has seen the Father."* Jesus came to earth to show a true reflection of the Father in heaven. All characteristics seen in Jesus are true about the Father as well (Hebrews 1:3).

Look up the traits of your new Father and fill in the blanks below with your findings:

Matthew 7:11 _____

_____

_____

Luke 12:30-32 _____

_____

_____

Luke 15:11-32 _____

_____

_____

_____

John 10:29_____

_____

_____

_____

John 14:2_____

_____

Ephesians 1:3-5 _____

_____

_____

_____

James 1:17 _____

_____

_____

_____

The privileges of being a son/daughter

Right before Jesus went to the cross to die for the sin of the world, He prayed an incredible prayer recorded in John 17. In verse 26 Jesus prayed to the Father, *"That the love with which You loved me may be in them, and I in them."*

Jesus actually prayed ahead for those who would later come to believe in Him. He prayed you would experience the same exact love that He personally shared with His Father. The love Jesus had from His Father was radical. In Luke 3:22, when Jesus was baptized by John the Baptist, heaven opened and the Father's voice was heard saying this, *"You are my beloved Son, in You I am well pleased."* This is the exact love believers get to experience as a child of God.

Change your concept about who God is if you see Him only as One who wants to punish and send people to hell. Check out these references: Matthew 18:14, John 3:15, 16 and 2 Peter 3:9. The Bible is clear that God is not willing for anyone to perish. By faith in Jesus and God's grace believers pass from death to life. There is no longer fear of hell. God is still to be feared in the sense of respect and honor for Him, but terror, shame, guilt or torment should be gone once you are His son or daughter. God is holy and does not take sin lightly, but coming into a new love relationship with Him will empower you to not want sin.

Read Romans 5:8. At what point in your life did God love you?

_____

_____

_____

This is crazy. As a son or daughter you are not loved based on your performance. God's love comes out of His heart and is not about what you do or don't do for Him. Even as you read earlier at Jesus' baptism, God declared His great love for His Son before Jesus did any miracles or preached any sermons. *God is love,* (1 John 4:16) and He loves because that is who He is. God's love for you is unconditional.

Read Romans 8:14-17. What do these verses say about the benefits of being a son/daughter of God? _____

_____

_____

_____

_____

_____

Did you catch that in Romans 8? You are a joint heir with Jesus Christ. Now that should make your day! Could you imagine being a joint heir with a child of the world's wealthiest family? As the Father treats Jesus, so He treats you. You are entitled to the same privileges as a child of God that Jesus is.

List some of the ways you think the Father treats Jesus. _____

_____

_____

_____

_____

Now remember, that all the things you just listed are the same way the heavenly Father treats you!

Action steps

1. List any negative views or lies you believed about God the Father due to circumstances or bad examples of authority.

   _____

   _____

   _____

   _____

2. List the truth of what God's Word says about who your Father in heaven is and what it means to be God's son in place of these lies. _____

   _____

   _____

3. If you have not already done so, forgive your earthly father for ways he failed you. Release your burden to the Lord. Don't allow an earthly father, no matter how good or bad he was, to take the place that only your Heavenly Father

can fulfill. Pray this through with your coach if needed.

4. Pray that by the work of the Holy Spirit, you would have a fresh experience with the great love of the Father. (See Romans 5:5)

5. Memorize John 1:12-13.

6. Read through the resources in the Appendix, *"Affirmations of Who I am in Christ."* Read it everyday and read it out loud. This will begin to help you line up with what God says about you.

Chapter 4

Seated in Heavenly Places

"But God, who is rich in mercy, because of His great love with which he loved us, even when we were dead in trespasses, made us alive together with Christ (by grace you have been saved), and raised us up together, and made us sit together in the heavenly places in Christ Jesus." Ephesians 2:4-6

When mankind passes from death to life, eternal life starts right away.

God speaks of your future as if it has already happened. Romans 8:30 says that, *"...those who are justified are already glorified."* The word "glorified" speaks of the state after death, when believers receive a new body in heaven. Obviously, once born again, life on earth does not cease to exist. If you are reading this, you have not yet been taken to heaven.

But there is a reality that when you become new, you hold a new residence in heaven right away.

Reigning in life

Who are the kings and priests?

Read Romans 5:17. What does this verse say about reigning? _

_____

_____

The word *reign*[3] means: to rule. When believers reign with Christ, it is in a position of authority. Jesus is the King of Kings and Jesus is the High Priest over salvation. Believers are not replacing Jesus here in any way. God has invited His children to share in His authority. The purpose of this authority is not to rule over others, but to influence the world to know Jesus and destroy the plans of the devil.

What does Revelation 5:9-10 say about this? _____

_____

_____

_____

_____

Kings

When Paul wrote his letters in the New Testament he often addressed them to "the church." For instance, in 1 Corinthians 1:2 the letter is addressed to *"the church of God."* The word "church" actually means an assembly. It is an assembling organization that has been delegated governing power by God.

Read Matthew 16:18-19. What is the purpose of the authority given by Jesus to the church? _____

_____

_____

_____

_____

Read 2 Corinthians 5:20. What is the function of a king or ambassador of Christ's kingdom? _____

_____

_____

_____

Believers are representatives of the King of kings, (just little "k" kings) but have been given great responsibility and authority. As you reign in your sphere of influence in life with Jesus, God calls you to represent (re-present) Christ. I encourage you to be reconciled to God. God has sent us, His church, into the world to show who He is so others might come to know Him in a personal relationship.

Read Matthew 10:1. How did Jesus send out the first representatives of the kingdom (His 12 disciples)?_____

_____

_____

_____

Priests

Read Hebrews 4:14-16. What do these scriptures reveal about Jesus? _____

_____

_____

_____

Since Jesus is your High Priest you are given access to God's throne at any time. This is unimaginable. A priest appointed by God in the Old Testament was to represent God's people

Israel before Him. In the books of Exodus and Leviticus, you can read about the tabernacle that hosted the Presence of God. His priests at the tabernacle offered sacrifices of animals for the sins of the people. The high priest could go into the Most Holy Place once a year on the Day of Atonement to offer sacrificial blood on the mercy seat of the Ark of the Covenant. It was in this Most Holy Place that the high priest experienced the real Presence of God.

Hebrews 10:14, says that *"For by one offering He (Jesus) has perfected forever those who are being sanctified."* Jesus' death on the cross was the blood sacrifice that now gives believers access into God's presence. You can go into God's presence any time, any day because Jesus offered His blood for you. This is an amazing privilege.

Not only are believers granted free access into God's presence but also are identified as priests as well. Read 1 Peter 2:9-10. What does this say about your priestly identity? _____

_____

_____

_____

_____

_____

As priests believers obviously don't offer animal sacrifices for the sins of people any longer. As you read earlier, kings are to represent God to people. Priests are to represent people to God. This is mainly done through your prayer life and relationship with God. As you pray and intercede for others, God will hear your prayers and work on their behalf.

Seated above the kingdom of darkness

Read Ephesians 1:20-23. Where is Christ seated? _____

_____

_____

_____

Believers are seated in heavenly places in Christ as you read earlier in Ephesians 2:6. This means that along with Jesus you are seated above the kingdom of darkness. You have a position of authority and have heaven's perspective. The next chapter will go into more depth on a believer's position of victory and authority in Christ over the devil's kingdom. The basis for the authority of a believer comes from the fact that he/she is already seated with Christ over the devil and has a sure hope of eternal life. Seated with Jesus, believers are positioned in authority over death, the devil and sin.

A heavenly perspective

Read Colossians 3:1-3. What do these verses reveal about someone who is seated with Christ? _____

_____

_____

_____

_____

_____

_____

A word of caution

To be clear, authority and reign that comes from being seated with Christ in heavenly places is not about superiority. The world does not need Christians who think they are better than everyone else. This is about a spiritual reality that empowers you to serve others in love. You have the privilege of seeing people come to Jesus through your reign in life. You reign above circumstances in your own life and over the plans of the devil. But people are to be served and honored, not ruled over. Use this freedom to be a blessing to others!

Action steps

1. How is God calling you to be an influence as a king and a priest? _____

   _____

   _____

   _____

2. Are there any situations in your life right now that you are approaching from a limited earthly perspective? _____

   _____

   _____

   _____

   _____

3. Since you now know that you are seated in heavenly places in Christ, how is God calling you to look at these situations from heaven's perspective? Pray about it and write down what God brings to your heart. _____

    _____

    _____

    _____

4. Memorize Ephesians 2:4-6.

5. Read through the appendix, *Affirmations of Who I am in Christ*. Read it everyday and read it out loud. This will begin to help you line up with what God says about you.

Chapter 5

Your Victory and Authority Over the Devil

"And the God of peace will crush Satan under your feet shortly."
Romans 16:20

Your enemy

You have an enemy: the devil and his kingdom (his demon assistants). You are in the midst of one world, but two realms. There is a spiritual realm and a natural realm. One realm is not more real than the other. The Bible teaches this and, if not seen in this context, life will be misinterpreted. Don't be overly consumed with the devil and demons, but be keenly aware of what they do and how God has given you victory over them.

The devil in the Bible has several names such as Satan, Lucifer, the father of lies, thief, deceiver, accuser, disguised as an angel of light and the list goes on. The devil once held a place of privilege as the angel Lucifer in heaven (Is. 14:12-15). But he became prideful and God kicked him out of his position. When this happened it was recorded in Revelation 12:4 that the devil took one third of the angels with him. These beings are referred to as demons or fallen angels.

The truth

Satan is not an equal with God. Here is a little comparison chart between God's kingdom and Satan's kingdom.

God	Satan
Creator	created
All-knowing	limited in knowledge
All-powerful	limited in power
All-present	limited presence in one location
Eternal	will be destroyed in the Lake of Fire
2/3 angels	1/3 demons
Love	hate
Originator	twister and manipulator
Light	darkness
Bright, glorious future	no future, no chance of redemption

What do God and Satan have in common? They both want you! They both want to put their identity upon your life. Let's unpack your new identity in Christ to reveal your position of victory and authority over the devil.

Your victory

Victory over the devil is completely tied to the victory Jesus won over the devil. Way back in the Garden of Eden the devil disguised himself as a serpent to trick man into disobeying God. This caused mankind to lose its true identity. God already foretold of the devil's demise. Read Genesis 3:14-15.

What is revealed about the devil's future demise? _____

_____

_____

In the New Testament it is clear: only through the cross of Jesus Christ is the devil defeated. Look up these scriptures and write down what they reveal about this powerful truth.

Colossians 2:13-15 _____

_____

_____

_____

1 John 3:8 _____

_____

Your authority

As seen in the last chapter, Christians are seated in heavenly places in Christ. This position in Christ is above the position of the kingdom of darkness (sometimes referred to in the Bible as principalities, powers, dominion, might, rulers and rulers of darkness. (See 1 Corinthians 2:8 and Ephesians 6:12). Those in Christ Jesus have been given authority over the devil's work. Read these scriptures below and write down what they reveal.

Matthew 10:1 _____

_____

_____

_____

_____

_____

Luke 10:18-20 _____

_____

_____

Romans 16:20 _____

_____

_____

_____

1 Corinthians 15:57 _____

_____

_____

_____

1 John 2:14 _____

_____

_____

_____

Authority from God does not come with a license to lord your power over people. His authority and victory are spiritual. This is not about being independent, rogue Christians that do whatever they want. Some people misunderstand authority. God has given you authority over the devil, but you still must stay under the authority of God. This means you still need to take orders from Him day to day and work where He is working. This isn't a free for all.

Winning in the battle

You have just read through some powerful scriptures about how the devil is defeated by Christ's victory and about how you share in that victory as well. The Bible is clear however that the devil is defeated, but not yet destroyed. Jesus said in Matthew 16:18-19, that hell will never prevail against the church. So have confidence based upon what Jesus did and what God's Word promises you. But the devil's complete destruction is coming in the future when God judges the world at the end of time. In Revelation 20:10 you can read that he will burn in the lake of fire and be tormented forever.

The devil mostly attacks and gains influence in the world through the minds of people. The next chapter will focus entirely on how to renew your mind.

What does 2 Corinthians 10:4-6 reveal about how the devil attacks and how believers overcome his attacks? _____

_____

_____

Look up these additional scriptures about the experience of warfare and how God has equipped believers to win the battle.

Matthew 16:18-19_____

_____

_____

Romans 13:12-14 _____

_____

_____

Ephesians 6:10-20 _____

_____

_____

_____

When the devil attacks your thoughts, through others and by temptation, God has called you to resist him. If this enemy addresses a Christian he is meant for humiliation and defeat. God is the One who gives victory, but He has called you to join Him in the experience of it all!

You may not be experiencing victory in your life due to various reasons. Here are some possible areas that can cause problems. Apply God's truth and possibly repent of:

- Wrong thinking

- Unbelief, or not fully believing God's promises

- Not taking your position of victory and authority in prayer

- Habitual sin

- Sexual immorality and soul ties

- Unforgiveness, bitterness, unhealthy anger

- Generational curses

- Not obeying God's Word

- Judgments

- Dabbling in other religions or idols

- Playing with occult games or objects

- Basing relationship with God on legalism (performance)

Action steps

Pray with your coach through any areas you think the devil may have a grip on you. Remember that unforgiveness can be one of the most toxic hindrances to your freedom in Christ. Make sure you deal with it if necessary. Below is a suggested prayer:

Father God,

I come to You in Jesus' name and ask that by Your Holy Spirit You would convict me of any sin in my life. I choose to confess the sins of _____ (whatever they are, take as much time as you need) and turn from them by Your grace. Jesus, thank You for Your blood shed on the cross for me. Thank You that Your blood is enough for all my sin to be forgiven and for me to be cleansed. Cleanse me from all unrighteousness. I renounce all the places I have given to the devil. I ask You to totally remove the devil's influence from me. I break the power of every curse, lie and sin against me in Jesus' name. I choose to forgive_____ (whoever they are, take as much time as you need) and ask You to remove the desire I have for them to be punished. I ask You to forgive me for being bitter toward others and empower me to love them like You do. I declare that whom Jesus sets free, is free indeed. Jesus, I give my whole life to You. Take away all my guilt and shame. Give me comfort and grace every day and lead me by Your Holy Spirit. Thank You for giving me victory over sin, the world and the devil. Thank You for raising Jesus from the dead and conquering death. Thank You for making me Your child. Father, fill me with Your love and with the Holy Spirit's power. In Jesus' name, Amen.

Do not try to dig for things in your life. Let the Holy Spirit reveal any areas you need to handle. Dealing with the devil is not difficult. He is not in a position of power when you come before God with a humble heart. Discovering and walking in your new identity in Christ and believing what God says are the main keys to sustaining your life of victory. This is done through a life of a love relationship with God mainly by prayer, worship and Bible reading. If you are stuck in an area, contact the church office and pick-up an "Application for Prayer Ministry." People will pray at length with you if you need freedom from the devil's grip.

1. Memorize Romans 16:20.

2. Read through the appendix, *"Affirmations of Who I am in Christ."* Read it everyday and read it out loud. This will begin to help you line up with what God says about you.

Chapter 6

Renew the Mind

"I beseech you therefore, brethren, by the mercies of God, that you present your bodies a living sacrifice, holy, acceptable to God, which is your reasonable service. And do not be conformed to this world, but be transformed by the renewing of your mind, that you may prove what is that good and acceptable and perfect will of God." Romans 12:1-2

Renewing your mind is about taking what you have learned and working it into your new life. God's promises are true at the moment you become born again when you are instantly accepted as God's child, but the learning process will take time. The process will help you develop your identity in Christ through faith in what God says. You may be thinking that some of the truths here, or laid out in the Bible, don't apply to your life, but don't allow your experience to define the Bible. Trust God that your life experience will be brought into harmony with God's Word.

In a way, your mind needs to catch up with what God has already done in your spirit and heart. So things are true about you in Christ, but they are not yet fully developed or realized. That does not make these things false, but it does mean that you need to allow yourself to grow into the fullness of what God says about you.

One of the reasons Paul wrote the book of Philippians was to correct the church at Philippi. They thought they had already arrived fully, were perfect and had no room to grow. The Apostle Paul, who wrote most of the New Testament, said in *Philippians 3:12, "Not that I have already attained, or am already perfected; but I press on, that I may lay hold of that for which Christ Jesus has also laid a hold of me."*

Change the way you think

The Bible teaches in *Proverbs 23:7, "..as a man thinks in his heart so is he."* The way you think determines your behavior. To change the way you live, you must change your thoughts.

What do these scriptures reveal about the process of renewing your mind? Look them up and write down what they reveal.

Romans 8:5-7 _____

_____

_____

_____

Philippians 4:8 _____

_____

_____

_____

Walk in the Spirit

The following scriptures reveal the process of renewing your mind. This happens by walking in the Spirit. When you walk with the Holy Spirit you will change the way you think and the way you live. You won't have to focus on or worry every day about what is right and wrong. The Holy Spirit will lead you. Read the verses and write down their truths.

Galatians 5:16-26 _____

_____

Ephesians 4:20-24 _____

_____

_____

_____

Colossians 3:2-10 _____

_____

_____

_____

Colossians 3:12-15 _____

_____

_____

Remember that you are dead

As you are in this process to renew your mind (which is life-long, by the way), you need to remind yourself that you are dead to your old life. It is still possible to sin as a Christian, but it should not be your regular behavior choice. 1 John 2:1, states believers purpose not to sin, but if you do, Jesus is there with the Father advocating for you to be cleansed and forgiven.

What does Romans 6:11-14 say about how your old way of life and sin must be handled? _____

_____

_____

_____

_____

You see you must remind yourself that you are dead. You must choose daily to submit your life to Jesus and thank Him for what He has done for you. You must choose an attitude that does not tolerate going back to a lifestyle that is already dead in Christ Jesus.

Obedience is a must

Read James 1:23-25. What is the warning in these verses?____

_____

_____

_____

If you only read God's Word and know what it says, but don't do what it says, you will forget who you are. Did you catch that? You will forget your identity. You must choose obedience to God's Word to renew your mind. Right thinking comes before right behavior. But right thinking does not replace the need to _do_ the right thing and obey.

Being a disciple of Jesus is a lifetime commitment. Your new identity comes right away with salvation, but being faithful to the process of walking in the Spirit and following Jesus is the only way to grow into maturity.

What does Luke 9:23-24 say Jesus instructs all to do? _____

_____

_____

_____

Where transformation begins

This isn't a formula, but these are things that must be in place to see genuine change.

- Walking in the Spirit - Galatians 5:16

- The Presence of God through the Holy Spirit – See 2 Corinthians 3:17-18

- Praying in the Spirit - Jude 20

- Bible reading and study that deepens relationship with Jesus – See John 5:39-40 (To discover the Person of Christ - not just words about Him.)

- Obedience to God's Word and His voice, which means a lifestyle of:

  o Being with the church to be around other believers - Hebrews 10:24-25

  o Receiving regular teaching - Acts 2:42

  o Choosing a disciplined lifestyle that includes personal prayer, worship and Bible reading - Matthew 6:6

  o Memorizing Bible verses - Matthew 4:4

  o Fasting and prayer - Matthew 6:17-18

Action steps

1. You need the Holy Spirit's help to renew your mind.

If you have not been baptized in the Holy Spirit and have not received the gift of tongues, pray with your coach. Receive tongues and start using your gift daily.

2. Do you feel God calling you to change any areas in your thinking? If so what are they? _____

_____

_____

_____

3. Right now are there any areas where God is calling for your obedience that have not been addressed? _____

_____

_____

_____

4. What is your plan to spend time with God? _____

_____

_____

_____

5. How does your plan need to change or grow? _____

_____

_____

6. Memorize Romans 12:1-2.

7. Read through the Appendix, *"Affirmations of Who I am in Christ."* Read it everyday and read it out loud. This will begin to help you line up with what God says about you.

Chapter 7

Healing and Miracles

"By His stripes we are healed." Isaiah 53:5

Healing

God has provided healing for your spirit, soul and body. The salvation discussed up to this point was about the spirit and soul. This chapter will be more about the body, but some of these truths apply to your soul as well.

Read Psalm 103:1-5. What does the Lord promise?_____

_____

_____

_____

Psalm 103 is an Old Testament scripture. Some have a hard time believing promises in the Old Testament. What does 2 Corinthians 1:20 say about the promises of God in Christ for you? _____

_____

_____

_____

In the Bible God has provided healing for spiritual issues and also physical issues. Often in the same breath Jesus promised both forgiveness of sin and healing of the body. You might separate these events in your mind and place spiritual needs over physical needs. Jesus deals with both. Read Luke 5:17-26. What happens in this story? _____

_____

_____

_____

It is through the cross that Jesus paid for healing. Read Isaiah 53:4-6. What do these verses promise? _____

_____

_____

_____

Read Matthew 8:16-17. Jesus confirmed this truth when he quoted this verse in connection with physical healing. What happened here? _____

_____

_____

_____

What does James 5:13-16 instruct you to do if you need healing?

_____

_____

_____

Miracles

Not only has Jesus provided healing but He calls believers to a life of the miraculous. God wants to use you to demonstrate who He is to the world through His healing and miracle power. What does Mark 16:17-18 say about you as a believer? _____

_____

_____

_____

Read Luke 10:9. What does Jesus say should go hand in hand when believers share the Good News of Jesus? _____

_____

_____

_____

Read Acts 1:8 and Acts 10:38. Where does the power come from, as seen in the life of Jesus, to accomplish miracles? _____

_____

_____

_____

God wants to use you to heal the sick, cast out demons and raise the dead. God can use you to do anything to extend His kingdom. He wants to use you. Don't follow after miracles, but miracles should follow you as a normal part of the Christian life. If you don't start praying for miracles, you won't see them in answer to your prayers. Step out and show God's love to others by praying for their needs. Don't be surprised when God does a miracle.

Some practical tips

- Sometimes people lose their healing. It's not that God doesn't finish a miracle, but Jesus warned in John 5:14 that sin can cause something to return or come back worse. So if you seek healing, stay away from sin and unbelief. Teach people to be thankful. Sometimes healing in the body is a process and not always immediate.

- Prayer and fasting increase the fruitfulness for healing. In Matthew 17:14-21, Jesus taught that a lifestyle of prayer and fasting was needed to break through in certain cases of healing. It appears, from this passage, that prayer and fasting help take unbelief out of the way for miracles to happen.

- Always minister to others in love. Don't define yourself or others by physical afflictions. The question why some get healed and others don't may not be answered unless God reveals it. The Apostle Paul was afflicted with no biblical record that he ever received a healing. Paul moved on and participated in the healing of many in Jesus' name. Jesus always encouraged people's faith to believe God for more. Don't beat up yourself or others emotionally if you are still waiting to see a miracle. Look for a way to encourage faith. Jesus paid a price for healing and for others to witness it. Don't lose heart!

Action steps

Pray for a miracle for your own needs and thank God for His provision.

1. Is there anyone God is calling you to pray for and lay hands on for a miracle? If so, who is it? _____

    _____

    _____

2. Memorize Isaiah 53:5.

3. Read Mark 6:1-6. Jesus was limited by people's unbelief. Ask God to remove any unbelief in your heart about what He can do, and repent. God loves you and wants to increase your faith. As you turn from unbelief and trust in God's Word your mind will be renewed as well.

4. Read through the appendix, *"Affirmations of Who I am in Christ."* Read it everyday and read it out loud. This will begin to help you line up with what God says about you.

Appendix

Who I am in Christ – The Identity, Authority, and Privileges I have as a New Creation

Read these daily in faith and read them out loud. This list is not exhaustive. You may find more during your own Bible reading and study.

These are Old Testament promises that are mine because I am in Christ (2 Corinthians 1:20).

1. God forgives all my iniquities and heals all my diseases (Psalm 103:3).

2. God redeems my life from destruction and crowns me with lovingkindness and tender mercies (Psalm 103:4)

3. God satisfies my mouth with good things and renews my youth like an eagle (Psalm 103:5).

4. God does not treat me as my sin deserves (Psalm 103:10).

5. God removes my sin as far as the east is from the west (Psalm 103:12).

6. I am known by God (Psalm 139:1).

7. I am fearfully and wonderfully made (Psalm 139:14).

8. God's thoughts toward me are precious and more in number than the sand (Psalm 139:17-18).

9. By the stripes of Jesus I am healed emotionally, physically and spiritually (Isaiah 53:4-5).

10. No weapon formed against me shall prosper (Isaiah 54:17).

11. God knew me before I was formed (Jeremiah 1:5).

12. God's plans for me are good. His plans are to give me a future and a hope (Jeremiah 29:11).

13. God has written His law on my heart and my mind (Jeremiah 31:33).

14. I have been given a new heart and a new spirit (Ezekiel 11:19).

15. God gave me a new heart and a new spirit, a heart of flesh for a heart of stone and His Spirit is within me to walk in His ways (Ezekiel 36:26-27).

16. God throws away my sin into the sea (Micah 7:19).

New Testament promises that are mine because I am in Christ

1. I have authority over all the power of the enemy (Luke 10:19).

2. I am loved by God (John 3:16).

3. I have been set free by the Truth (John 8:31-32).

4. I am held in my Father God's hand and no one can snatch me away (John10:29).

5. I am dead to sin (Romans 6:2-11).

6. Sin shall not be master over me (Romans 6:14).

7. I am a child of God (Romans 8:16).

8. I am more than a conqueror through Jesus who loves me (Romans 8:37).

9. I am loved by Jesus (Romans 8:38-39).

10. My body is a temple of the Holy Spirit (1 Corinthians 6:19).

11. I was bought at a price (1 Corinthians 6:20).

12. I am in Christ (2 Corinthians 5:17).

13. I am a new creation (2 Corinthians 5:17).

14. I am redeemed (Galatians 3:13).

15. I have been crucified to the world and the world crucified to me (Galatians 6:14).

16. I have been adopted, chosen and accepted by Father God (Ephesians 1:3-6).

17. I have redemption through Christ's blood, forgiveness of sins (Ephesians 1:7).

18. I have an inheritance in Christ (Ephesians 1:11).

19. I have been sealed with the Holy Spirit of promise (Ephesians 1:13-14).

20. I have been made alive together with Christ (Ephesians 2:4-5).

21. I have been saved by grace through faith and not by works (Ephesians 2:8-9).

22. I am God's workmanship, His poem (Ephesians 2:10).

23. I am a citizen of heaven (Philippians 3:20).

24. I am in the Kingdom of the Son of God's love (Colossians 1:13).

25. I am out of the kingdom of darkness (Colossians 1:13).

26. Christ is in me, the hope of glory (Colossians 1:27).

27. I have been made alive together with Jesus and forgiven of all my trespasses (Colossians 2:13).

28. I have been raised with Christ (Colossians 3:3).

29. I am the elect of God, holy, and beloved (Colossians 3:12).

30. I have not been given a spirit of fear, but of power, love and a sound mind (2 Timothy 1:7).

What is the next step?

You may be able to continue your discipleship studies with the same person who helped you work through this book. If you need to transition to another person, please allow your pastors to assist you and help you stay connected. It is a very high priority for leaders to be sure you are connected in order to finish your discipleship.

Review this book, *A New Identity*

Review this book on your own to establish these new patterns. Coaches, disciplers, pastors and teachers are always available to answer questions as they arise.

Utilize the New Believers' Series

1. *The New Birth and the New Life,* by Scott Smith & John Hammer

2. *A New Identity The Identity, Authority and Privileges we have in Christ,* by John Hammer

3. *Contagious Discipleship,* by Dr. Dan Hammer & Doug Martin

4. *Gifts of the Spirit*, by Dr. Dan Hammer

Read these to help you grow

Here is a list of additional resources you will find valuable on your journey.

Who We Are in Christ, by Joe McIntyre

The Authority of the Believer, by Che Ahn

Equipmentor Series, by Dr. Dan Hammer

Intimate Friendship with God, by Joy Dawson

Be equipped

As leaders of the Body of Christ one goal is to equip the saints for the work of the ministry.

You are a disciple of Jesus. As you grow and mature you will come to a place of strength in your relationship with God.

See the evidence

Here is proof that shows you are strong and established in your faith:

Daily authentic relationship with God

Daily prayer time

Daily Word time

Practicing witness for Jesus

Faithful in the house of God

Submitted to leadership

Obedient to scripture

You will be ready to help make disciples of others who make Jesus their Lord and Savior. This may seem impossible to you right now, but the people discipling you were once discipled themselves.

Stay connected

We are here to help you every step of the way. You will succeed. Jesus is praying for you (Hebrews 7:25)

I can do all things through Christ who strengthens me. (Philippians 4:13)

References

1. Strong, James, "Sanctified," *The New Strong's Exhaustive Concordance of the Bible,* Nashville, © Thomas Nelson, 1996 Print.

2. Strong, James,"Justified," *The New Strong's Exhaustive Concoradace of the Bible*, Nashville © Thomas Nelson, 1996, Print.

3. Strong James, "Reign," *The New Strong's Exhaustive Concordance of the Bible*, Nashville © Thomas Nelson, 1996, Print.

Made in the USA
San Bernardino, CA
07 October 2017